AMAZING
STRUCTURES

Amazing
Unusual
Structures

CAROLINE THOMAS

REDBACK
publishing

Redback Publishing
PO Box 357 Frenchs Forest NSW 2086
Australia

www.redbackpublishing.com.au
orders@redbackpublishing.com.au

ISBN 978-1-925860-91-7

Author: Caroline Thomas
Designer: Redback Publishing

Originated by Redback Publishing
Printed and bound in Malaysia

Acknowledgements
Abbreviations: l—left, r—right, b—bottom, t—top, c—centre, m—middle
We would like to thank the following for permission to reproduce photographs: (Images © shutterstock), p4tl, p20 VIKVAD, p4bl, p9tl, p31tl renatopmeireles, p4tr, p13tr, p31bcl Rudy Mareel, p4mr, p7tr, p30tl TTstudio, p5tl, p10-11, p30tcr Lipskiy, p5bl, p31bl Catalin Lazar, p5tr, p23 Maykova Galina, p5mr, p31bcr Songquan Deng, p5bl, p26, p31br Wade Machin, p6tl Natata, p8tl Unknown (Mondadori Publishers), Public domain, via Wikimedia Commons, p8-9m Diego Grandi, p10tl Hannes Grobe, CC BY-SA 2.5 (https://creativecommons.org/licenses/by-sa/2.5) via Wikimedia Commons, p10bl, p30tr Herbert Schwingenschlögl, CC BY-SA 3.0 (http://creativecommons.org/licenses/by-sa/3.0/), via Wikimedia Commons, p11tr Evannovostro, p12 tl DFree, p12mr Sophie James, p12bc lulu and isabelle, p13ml Torben Knauer, p13br telesniuk, p14-15m, p31tc cowardlion, p15tr Sean Pavone, p16-17 Richie Chan, p16ml Eastimages, p17tr maoyunping, p18, p31tr cowardlion, p19 XIE CHENGXIN, p19cl CC BY-SA 3.0 (https://commons.wikimedia.org/wiki/File: bi4 disc.jpg), p20tl spatuletail, p20br Jeffrey Neal at the English Wikipedia, CC BY-SA 3.0 (http://creativecommons.org/licenses/by-sa/3.0/), via Wikimedia Commons, p21 Artur Jakucewicz, p21tr Luna2631, p22m ABIR ROY BARMAN, p22tl Vibgyor Studios, p24bl, p30bc Willowtreehouse, p24mc Sue Leighton, p24tr ennerodesign, p24mr Michael Major, p24br neftali, p25tl SimonTFL, CC BY-SA 3.0 (https://creativecommons.org/licenses/by-sa/3.0), via Wikimedia Commons, p25ml Whinging Pom, CC BY-SA 2.0 (https://creativecommons.org/licenses/by-sa/2.0), via Wikimedia Commons, p25bl Michael Coghlan from Adelaide, Australia, CC BY-SA 2.0 (https://creativecommons.org/licenses/by-sa/2.0), via Wikimedia Commons, p25mt Alex Cimbal, p25mb Stuart Edwards, Public domain, via Wikimedia Commons, p25tr myphotobank.com.au, p25mr cn2480.com.au, CC BY-SA 3.0 (https://creativecommons.org/licenses/by-sa/3.0), via Wikimedia Commons, p25br crbellette, p27 myphotobank.com.au, p28mr Nick-D, CC BY-SA 3.0 (https://creativecommons.org/licenses/by-sa/3.0), via Wikimedia Commons, p30bl Jorge Franganillo, CC BY 2.0, p30br Annette Teng, CC BY 3.0 (https://creativecommons.org/licenses/by/3.0), via Wikimedia Commons

Contents

AMAZING
STRUCTURES

UNUSUAL

North
America

Central
America

U.K.

3

4

South
America

Modern Landmarks Key

1. **Fallingwater, USA**
2. **Niterói Contemporary Art Museum, Brazil**
3. **Guggenheim Museum Bilbao, Spain**
4. **Sagrada Família, Spain**
5. **Hundertwasser House, Austria**
6. **Lotus Temple, India**
7. **Genghis Khan Equestrian Statue, Mongolia**
8. **Beijing National Stadium, China**
9. **SAHMRI Building, Australia**
10. **The Bahá'í House of Worship, Australia**

All over the world, people have built structures, buildings and whole cities that can amaze and inspire. People travel far and wide to marvel at these incredible structures, admiring their beauty or innovation, as well as the manpower and tenacity it took to create them.

LANDMARKS

Europe

5

Middle East

Africa

7

Asia

8

6

Australia

9

10

One Vision, Many Hands

Many of these structures were the vision of
one person, but built by many. In modern
times, **architects** and **engineers** are artists,
using steel and **concrete** as their canvas.
They create enormous works of art in cities
all over the world.

ANTONI GAUDÍ

Antoni Gaudí was a Spanish architect who was a practitioner of Catalan Modernism. His work was free-flowing and greatly influenced by nature. Most of his designs are in Barcelona and are described as highly unique.

Seven properties built by Gaudí, in or near Barcelona are UNESCO Heritage Sites, together listed as The Works of Antoni Gaudí.

1. Casa Batlló
2. Casa Milà
3. Casa Vicens
4. Crypt in Colònia Güell
5. Gaudí's work on the Nativity facade and Crypt of La Sagrada Família
6. Parc Güell
7. Palau Güell

Casa Milà, also known as La Pedrera

La Pedrera was built between 1906 and 1912. It is a residential building with a wave-shaped stone exterior. It has 32 unique, abstract iron balcony fences that include animal and plant-like shapes. UNESCO recognised this building as a World Heritage Site in 1984.

Sagrada Família

The most famous of all Gaudí's works has been under construction since the first stone was laid in 1882. The original architect, Francisco de Paula del Villar y Lozano, had disagreements about the building, so resigned and the job fell to Antoni Gaudí. He worked for 43 years on the temple until his death in1926.

It is scheduled to be completed in 2026, on the 100th anniversary of the architect's death. In 2005, **UNESCO** declared the Sagrada Família a **World Heritage Site**.

Parc Güell

One of Gaudí's major works, Parc Güell, was built between 1900 and 1914. Parc Güell is a garden complex that contains amazing stone structures, beautiful ceramic tiling and fascinating buildings, including Gaudí's house. UNESCO declared the garden a World Heritage Site in 1984.

The main terrace has a long bench in the shape of a snake, decorated with colourful tiles. Below this terrace there is a large hall, held up with many columns that are meant to mimic a forest. A fountain at the entrance to Güell Park includes a large sculpted dragon.

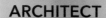OSCAR NIEMEYER

Oscar Ribeiro de Almeida Niemeyer Soares Filho (December 15, 1907 – December 5, 2012) was a Brazilian architect. Over his life, he created a large portfolio of architecture, sculpture and furniture. He also worked with other architects to design the headquarters of the United Nations in New York. He is most famous for the design of the civic buildings in Brasília, a planned city that in 1960 became the capital of Brazil.

Brasília became an experimental canvas a for the visionary architect and in 1987, the city became a UNESCO World Heritage site.

The Niterói Contemporary Art Museum

The Niterói Contemporary Art Museum in Rio de Janeiro was constructed on the cliffs that overlook Guanabara Bay. It offers beautiful views of the water and Sugarloaf Mountain. Oscar Niemeyer and structural engineer Bruno Contarini designed the museum to look like a flying saucer hovering above the bay. The four-storey structure took five years to build, with 300 workers taking turns over three shifts.

The building measures 50 metres in diameter and covers an area of nearly two thousand square metres. Its support beams were built using prestressed concrete and the circular roof was given special heat treatment and waterproofing. It was finished in 1996.

Oscar Niemeyer's Brasília buildings include:

- The Planalto Palace: the official office of the President
- The Monumental Axis
- The Cathedral of Brasília
- The National Museum of the Republic
- The National Congress of Brazil
- Itamaraty Palace: The Ministry of External relations
- The Brasília Palace Hotel
- The Palace of the Dawn

HUNDERTWASSER

Born in Vienna as Friedrich Stowasser, Hundertwasser was an artist and designer who had a passion for spirals and flowing lines. First known as a successful artist, he entered the field of architecture in the 1950s.

Hundertwasser designed many unusual structures around the world including a church and a day-care centre in Frankfurt, Germany. He even designed a toilet block in New Zealand.

Kunst Haus Wien

Kunst Haus Wien is a museum in Vienna that was designed by Hundertwasser and which houses the world's only permanent exhibition of Hundertwasser's works. Temporary exhibitions of other artists are also displayed in the museum.

Built in 1892 and renovated from 1989 to 1991, the building design includes lots of wavy lines, typical of the artist's style. There are bright colours throughout and an uneven, winding staircase leading to the upper floors. It has a total exhibition area of 4,000 square metres.

Hundertwasser Village

Opposite the Hundertwasserhaus is the Hundertwasser Village, which is open to visitors. Hundertwasser created the village in a tyre workshop between 1990 and 1991. There are a number of stores, cafes and bars in the typical Hundertwasser style.

Hundertwasser House

The Hundertwasser House in Vienna is one of Austria's top tourist attractions and an architectural highlight. This apartment block contains 53 apartments, four offices, 16 private terraces and three communal terraces.

The Hundertwasserhaus is designed with wavy lines, uneven windows and a colourful, patchwork exterior. Hundertwasser even planned to have uneven floors, but for practical reasons, this didn't happen. Construction began on the public housing building in 1983 and was completed in 1985. It quickly became a popular destination for locals and tourists, with its 200 trees and shrubs planted on its balconies and roof. The Hundertwasser House is a colourful, chaotic oasis of nature and art in the city.

FRANK GEHRY

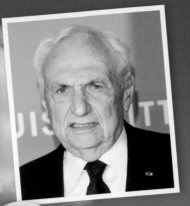

Frank Gehry is a Canadian-born American architect, living in Los Angeles. In the past fifty years, he has built dozens of unusual and controversial buildings all over the world.

Weisman Art Museum, Minneapolis, USA

The Weisman Art Museum overlooks the Mississippi River and was completed in 1993. The building has two contrasting sides, a brick facade that blends with the nearby historic buildings and a shiny, brushed steel side that is an abstraction of a waterfall and a fish. The museum received a major expansion, designed by Frank Gehry, in 2011.

Vitra Design Museum, Weil am Rhein, Germany

Gehry's Vitra Design Museum opened in 1989. It is a work of deconstructivism, geometric forms, towers, ramps and cubes.

Guggenheim Museum Bilbao, Spain

Gehry's Guggenheim Museum Bilbao is one of the great buildings of the 20th Century. It is his most famous work and the one that secured his place among the world's greatest architects. Completed in 1997, it is more like sculpture than architecture, with interconnecting shapes of stone, glass and titanium on a 32,500 square metre site. The museum has been a major catalyst for economic development, bringing tens of millions of visitors to the city.

Dancing House, Prague, Czech Republic

The Nationale-Nederlanden building is mostly known as the 'Dancing House' or 'Fred and Ginger', thanks to its signature pair of towers, which seem to resemble a couple dancing. It is one of the most significant landmarks in Prague. This 3,000-square-metre space is used as offices, a restaurant, a gallery, a conference centre and a sightseeing terrace. Constructed in 1996, the building consists of metal mesh, glass and concrete. It was created in collaboration between Gehry and local architect Vlado Miluníc.

Neuer Zollhof, Düsseldorf, Germany

Gehry's Düssledorf structure consists of three contrasting building complexes. The different materials chosen give each complex its own identity. The building complex looks like a gigantic sculpture.

THE NATIONAL CENTRE FOR THE PERFORMING ARTS

Construction Materials

The dome measures 212 metres in an east-west direction, 143 metres in a north-south direction and towers 46 metres high. The exterior consists of over 18,000 titanium plates and over 1,000 sheets of ultra-white glass. Construction began in December 2001 and the inaugural concert was held in December 2007.

Beijing's National Centre for the Performing Arts (NCPA) is an arts centre and opera house. Designed by French architect Paul Andreu, this unusual building seats 5,452 people across three halls. The centre is a 12,000-square-metre, ellipsoid dome, which earns the structure its nickname, The Egg. It is surrounded by a 35,500-square-metre artificial lake.

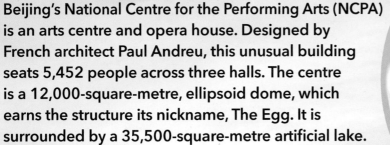

Transparent Underpass

To maximise the egg-shape illusion, there is only one way to get in or out of the building, a 60-metre long transparent underpass. This passageway is intended to transport the public out of the ordinary day-to-day and into a space where creativity, fiction and entertainment can begin.

Crystal Clear

The artificial lake is an important part of the building design. It is required to create the reflections that make the important egg-shape stand out against the rectangular buildings that surround it. To keep this illusion working all year round, the lake is engineered so that it never freezes over and that the water always remains crystal clear.

BEIJING NATIONAL STADIUM

Real Steel

The Bird's Nest is the largest steel structure in the world, occupying 255,000 square metres and requiring 42,000 tonnes of steel for its construction. The steel lattice design gives the building an organic, woven look that contrasts against the mostly rectangular city buildings nearby. Whilst many see the lattice as an irregular series of strung lines, there are many overlapping pentagons that replicate the stars on the National Flag of the People's Republic of China, also known as the Five-star Red Flag.

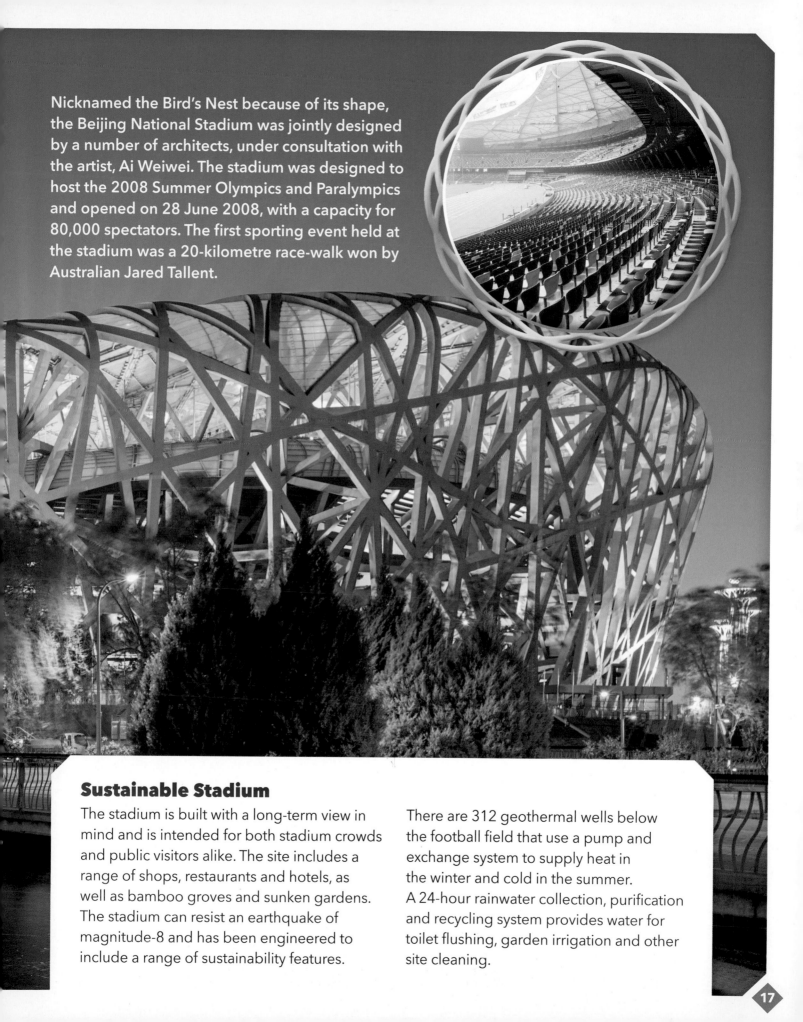

Nicknamed the Bird's Nest because of its shape, the Beijing National Stadium was jointly designed by a number of architects, under consultation with the artist, Ai Weiwei. The stadium was designed to host the 2008 Summer Olympics and Paralympics and opened on 28 June 2008, with a capacity for 80,000 spectators. The first sporting event held at the stadium was a 20-kilometre race-walk won by Australian Jared Tallent.

Sustainable Stadium

The stadium is built with a long-term view in mind and is intended for both stadium crowds and public visitors alike. The site includes a range of shops, restaurants and hotels, as well as bamboo groves and sunken gardens. The stadium can resist an earthquake of magnitude-8 and has been engineered to include a range of sustainability features.

There are 312 geothermal wells below the football field that use a pump and exchange system to supply heat in the winter and cold in the summer. A 24-hour rainwater collection, purification and recycling system provides water for toilet flushing, garden irrigation and other site cleaning.

CMG HEADQUARTERS

Also called the CCTV Building, the headquarters of China Media Group is 54 storeys high. Its geometric design creates a loop shape, with two 'L' shaped buildings connecting at their top and bottom. Construction started in June 2004 and was completed in May 2012.

Construction Challenges

The design and construction were challenging because of the building's unusual shape and its location in a seismic zone. Beijing's extreme weather conditions had to be taken into consideration when joining the two sections of the building together, as the structure expands and contracts in hot and cold weather.

In 2013, it won the Best Tall Building Worldwide Award from the Council on Tall Buildings and Urban Habitat.

GUANGZHOU CIRCLE

Guangzhou Circle houses the world's largest stock exchange for raw plastic material. It is the world's tallest circular building, towering 138 metres above Guangzhou in southern China. It was opened in 2013, with 33 storeys and 85,000 square metres of floor area.

Ancient Jade discs inspired the building's design

Architect's Inspiration

Guangzhou Circle was designed by Italian architect Joseph di Pasquale. He was inspired by a number of Chinese symbols including a coin, a feng shui symbol and the insignia of the royal dynasty that reigned in the area 2,000 years ago.

FALLINGWATER

FRANK LLOYD WRIGHT

2c U.S. POSTAGE

Architect: Frank Lloyd Wright

Frank Lloyd Wright is considered to be one of the forerunners of Classical Modernism and America's most esteemed architect. He designed Fallingwater in 1934 for his clients, the Kaufmann family. The house became famous and is now a natural historic landmark in Pennsylvania. The Kaufmanns' love for the property's waterfalls inspired Wright to place the house across from the falls, to merge with nature. The interior is designed to resemble nature.

A National Historic Landmark

Construction of Fallingwater ended in 1937 and the Kaufmann family began using it as their weekend retreat. In 1963, the conservation of the home was entrusted to the Western Pennsylvania Conservancy and the home was opened to the public. Today, the house retains its original furniture and receives thousands of visitors per year. In 1976, Fallingwater became a National Historic Landmark in the US.

CUBE HOUSES

The Cube Houses are one of Rotterdam's most innovative and iconic attractions. Designed by Dutch architect Piet Blom, these homes are cubes that are tilted by 45 degrees. They were designed asymmetrically to resemble an abstract forest with each triangular roof representing a treetop. There are 38 small cubes and two 'super-cubes' all attached to each other.

THE LOTUS TEMPLE

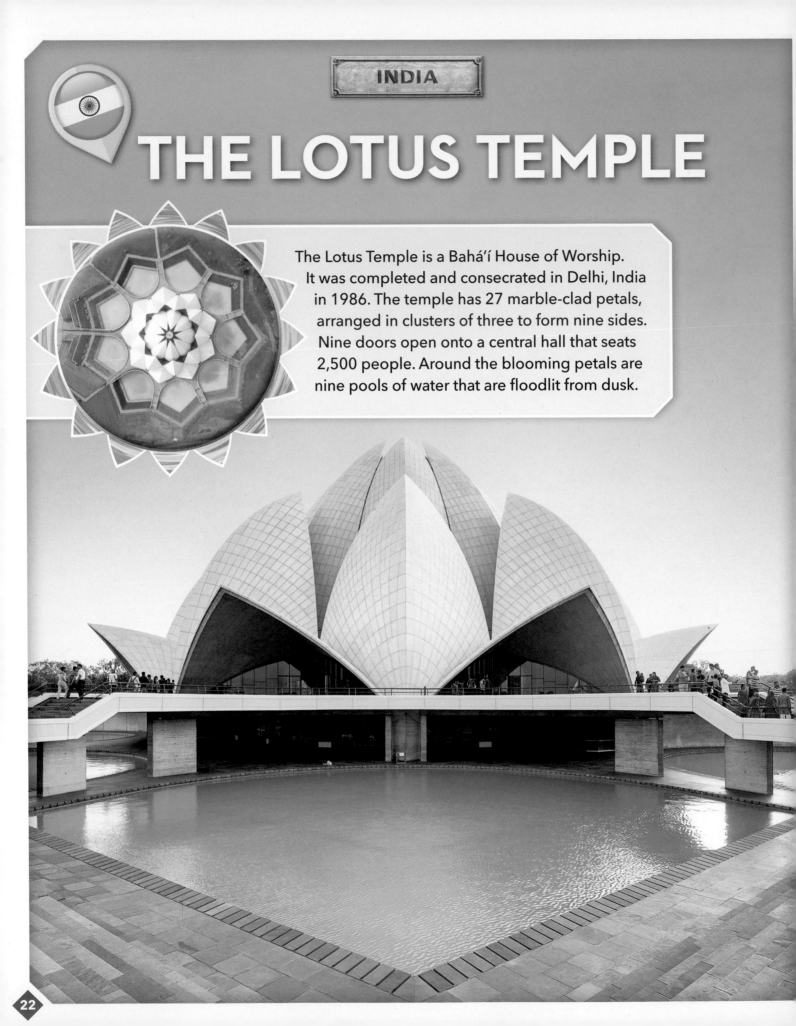

The Lotus Temple is a Bahá'í House of Worship. It was completed and consecrated in Delhi, India in 1986. The temple has 27 marble-clad petals, arranged in clusters of three to form nine sides. Nine doors open onto a central hall that seats 2,500 people. Around the blooming petals are nine pools of water that are floodlit from dusk.

GENGHIS KHAN EQUESTRIAN STATUE

Genghis Khan is remembered as a brutal conqueror, but in Mongolia he is a national hero who founded the Mongol Empire. On the bank of the Tuul River, 54 kilometres east of the Mongolian capital Ulaanbaatar, a great statue has been constructed in his honour. It is the tallest statue of a man on horseback in the world.

Steed of Steel

This huge stainless steel statue was built in 2008 to celebrate the 800th anniversary of the **foundation** of the Mongolian Empire and to honour its founder, Genghis Khan. The structure is 40 metres high and weighs 226 tonnes. Visitors can go up the statue to the head of the horse, using an elevator or stairs.

Australia's BIG THINGS

There are more than 150 very unusual structures around Australia, in every state and territory. Some of these big things are novelty architecture while others are sculptures.

Humpty Doo
Darwin

NORTHERN TERRITORY

Alice Springs

WESTERN AUSTRALIA

Perth

Hopetoun

THE BIG GALAH

The Big Banana, Coffs Harbour

KINGSTON SE

AUSTRALIA 50c

Fun Family Road Trips

Australia's fascination with these large, weird structures began in the 1960s when statues such as Adelaide's Big Scotsman and the Big Banana in Coffs Harbour were opened. Suddenly family road trips became fun. Now you can't drive very far is this vast country without being able to spot a 'big thing'.

THE BIG CASSOWARY

Mission Beach

QUEENSLAND

SOUTH AUSTRALIA

The Big Lobster, Kingston

THE BIG PRAWN

Woombye
Brisbane
Gold Coast
Balina
Coffs Harbour

THE GIANT MURRAY COD

Kimba

NEW SOUTH WALES

Tamworth

THE BIG BANANA
COFFS HARBOUR

Sydney
Goulburn

Adelaide

Canberra
ACT

Swan Hill

Kingston

VICTORIA

Melbourne

THE BIG PLATYPUS

Latrobe

Penguin

The Big Merino, Goulburn

SAHMRI BUILDING

Adelaide's SAHMRI Building has been nicknamed the 'Spaceship' and the 'Cheese Grater'. It is a bold, innovative structure that accommodates up to 675 health and medical researchers.

Inspired by Nature

Designed by architectural firm Woods Bagot, Adelaide's SAHMRI Building opened in November 2013. The building cost $200 million dollars, takes up approximately 25,000 square metres of space and consists of 6,290 triangular glass panels. The facade was inspired by the skin of a pinecone to act as a sunshade, while maintaining views and daylight. Inside, there are curved white walls and 15,000 triangular windows.

RUNDLE LANTERN

The Rundle Lantern in Adelaide is a spectacular light show attached to the Adelaide City Council's Rundle Street car park. This nine-storey Lantern is made up of 748 square LED panels that are controlled by a central computer. It is 100 per cent green-powered and carbon neutral. What was once an ordinary car park is now a spectacular light show and top tourist attraction.

SHINE DOME

Canberra's Shine Dome, previously known as Becker House, is sometimes referred to as 'The Martian Embassy', both because of its shape and the foreign embassies it shares a city with.

Shine Dome is surrounded by a moat

Historical Significance

The Shine Dome was designed by architect Sir Roy Grounds in 1956 and construction was completed in 1959. At the time, it was Australia's largest dome building.

The concrete is approximately 60 centimetres thick at its base and 10 centimetres thick at the top. The 45.75-metre diameter dome supports itself, with no internal wall holding it up. It was the first building in Canberra to be added to the National Heritage List, for its historical and architectural significance.

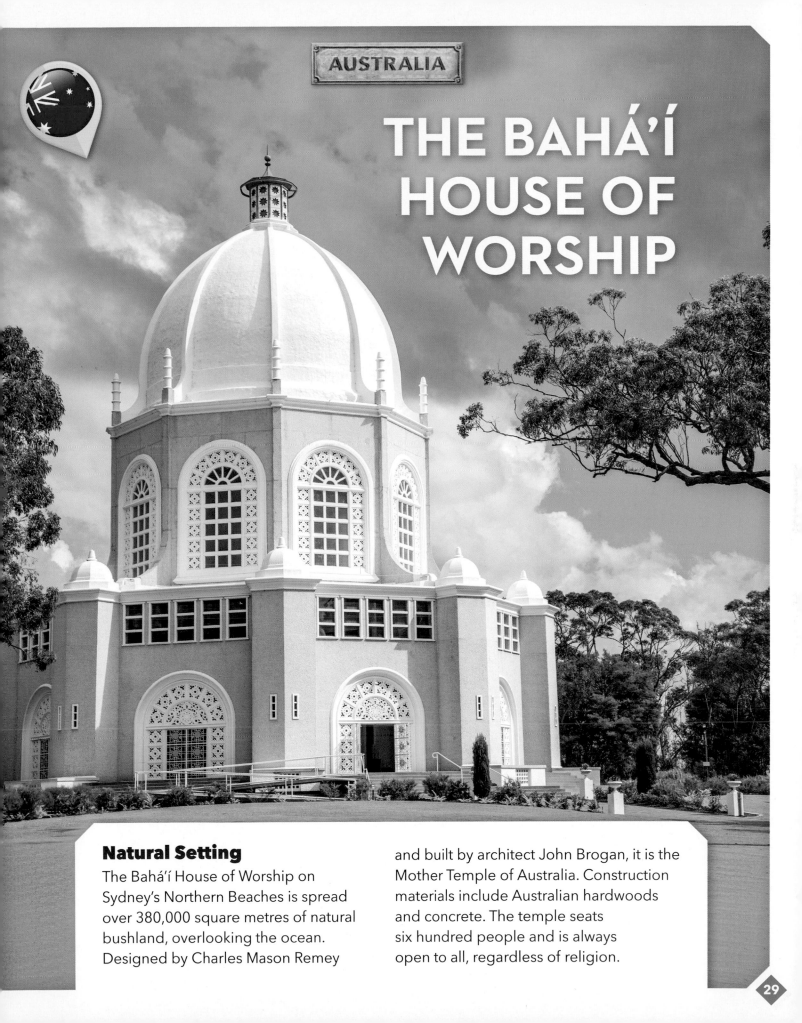

THE BAHÁ'Í HOUSE OF WORSHIP

Natural Setting

The Bahá'í House of Worship on Sydney's Northern Beaches is spread over 380,000 square metres of natural bushland, overlooking the ocean. Designed by Charles Mason Remey and built by architect John Brogan, it is the Mother Temple of Australia. Construction materials include Australian hardwoods and concrete. The temple seats six hundred people and is always open to all, regardless of religion.

Unusual STRUCTURES

1882
The first stone was laid at Sagrada Família in Barcelona, Spain

1959
The Shine Dome opens in Canberra, Australia

1985
Hundertwasser House opens in Vienna, Austria

1989-1991
Kunst Haus Wien is renovated in Vienna, Austria

1900-1914
Parc Güell was built in Barcelona, Spain

1964
The Big Banana opens in Coffs Harbour, Australia

1988
The Big Golden Guitar opens in Tamworth, Australia

TIMELINE

1996
The Niterói Contemporary Art Museum is finished in Niterói, Brazil

2007
The National Centre for the Performing Arts, Beijing, China held its Inaugural Concert

2012
The CMG CCTV Headquarters opens in Beijing, China

1996
The Lotus Temple opens and is consecrated in Delhi, India

1997
The Guggenheim Museum opens in Bilbao, Spain

2008
The Beijing National Stadium opens in China

2013
The SAHMRI Building opens in Adelaide, Australia

Index

Glossary

architect .... person who designs a building

concrete .... blend of sand, cement, gravel and water used as a building material

engineer .... person who analyses and designs a building's support elements in order to make it safe

foundation .... part of a building beneath ground level that transfers the building's weight to the earth

UNESCO World Heritage Site .... site designated by the United Nations to be of worth to the world